Original title:
Jade Plant Dreams

Copyright © 2025 Creative Arts Management OÜ
All rights reserved.

Author: Isaac Ravenscroft
ISBN HARDBACK: 978-1-80581-893-9
ISBN PAPERBACK: 978-1-80581-420-7
ISBN EBOOK: 978-1-80581-893-9

Glimpses into Photosynthetic Whimsy

In a pot, a green delight,
With leaves like coins, shining bright.
It dances in the sunlight's sway,
Oh, what mischief it might play!

Gazing wide, I see it grin,
A quirky look, the fun begins.
A garden party, tiny tease,
With whispers carried by the breeze.

Planted dreams in muddy clay,
Who knew they'd sprout such wacky play?
With every stretch, a little tease,
It knows how to bring me to my knees.

The neighbors think it's quite absurd,
As I chat sweet nonsense, so unheard.
But, oh, the jokes it tells at night,
They make the moonbeam giggle bright!

Verdant Whispers of Delight

In a pot there sits a green delight,
Winking leaves in morning light.
A tiny tree with dreams so grand,
Telling jokes, unplanned and bland.

It sways with laughter, roots so bold,
Telling tales of soil and gold.
Cactus friends can't join the fun,
They prickly frown, but we just run.

Nurtured by Nature's Touch

My leafy friend, so full of cheer,
Dances happily, year to year.
With a sprinkle of love and just a touch,
It giggles softly; thank you very much!

Once a month, I feed it bright,
It loves to munch in sheer delight.
Fertilizer friends, oh what a joke,
They laugh with me, then go up in smoke!

The Elixir of Life in Petals

Sipping sunlight, leaves so fine,
A cocktail party, oh divine!
With bubbles made of carbon bliss,
It raises a glass; you can't miss this!

Roots beneath, the party starts,
Dancing dandelions in leafy carts.
Each leaf a sip of laughter flows,
Tickling toes as the sunlight glows.

Embracing the Succulent Dream

In dreamland lush, our stories thrive,
Succulent shenanigans come alive.
With a wink and a twist, they tease away,
Chasing the bugs that dare to stay.

A little drip from a watering can,
Turns my home into some green lan.
Oh, to be a leaf on that joyous spree,
In a pot, forever wild and free!

Eden Encased in Glass

In a pot, a world so small,
Tiny creatures dance and crawl.
Leaves whisper secrets, tales so grand,
Inside this glass, it's all well planned.

A cactus grins, a flower stares,
Who knew plants could have such flares?
The light shines bright on this green land,
A kingdom grand, by nature's hand.

Guardians of the Indoor Sanctuary

With spiky crowns and leafy capes,
They guard the realm of winding tapes.
Chasing dust with a gentle sway,
Who knew plants could save the day?

Each fern a knight, each sprout a squire,
In pots they plot, they never tire.
When shadows loom and dims the light,
They cheer you up, your leafy knights.

The Language of Living Soil

Speak to the dirt, it knows your name,
A whispered wish, a secret game.
The roots reply with a subtle tease,
In this rich world, they aim to please.

The shovels dance, the rakes do sing,
As worms compose a lively spring.
A symphony beneath our feet,
In every pot, life's rhythm beats.

Petite Leaves, Grand Aspirations

Tiny leaves, with dreams so big,
They reach for stars, they dance a jig.
A mini forest, a thriving crew,
In every corner, life anew.

They plot to grow, they scheme to spread,
With every inch, their dreams are fed.
In laugh and cheer, they sprout and bloom,
These little ones will take the room.

Softer Than Air

In the corner, so spry and bright,
A green buddy, a true delight.
With leaves that twist, dance, and sway,
It giggles softly throughout the day.

When I water, it whispers cheer,
'Not too much, my friend, have no fear!'
A sprinkle here, a splash here and there,
My leafy pal shows it does care.

Stronger Than Stone

With roots that grip like a stubborn pet,
It stands its ground, no hint of regret.
Not swayed by winds or the morning sun,
This green wonder rolls on, just having fun.

Neighbors wonder, 'What's its secret?'
'The more you stare, the less you get!'
But in its silence, it grows and beams,
Confident in its leafy dreams.

Vitality in Every Vein

A burst of green in the morning light,
It peeks at me, what a funny sight!
With every sip, it loves to boast,
'I'm thriving here, coast to coast!'

The bugs pass by, a bit confused,
'How can this plant be so well-fused?'
Its charm and glee, a lively show,
In every vein, vitality flows.

The Muse of Evocative Green

Sitting still, yet full of jest,
It inspires the best, leaves none depressed.
With a wink, it shares stories untold,
Of dreams spun in sunlight, bold yet old.

When shadows creep in, it plays a trick,
A flash of green, quick and slick.
'Chase away gloom, let's have a laugh!'
In this quirky show, I'm but its gaffe.

A Symphony of Succulent Breath

With whispers soft, it hums a tune,
A melody crafted beneath the moon.
With every breeze, it joins the dance,
In the world of greens, it takes a chance.

Each leaf a note, in harmony,
Creating joy, just wait and see!
'Be happy now, don't let it fade,'
In my lovely plant, I'm serenely played.

Lush Whispers of Serenity

In a pot so round and green,
A tiny tree with leaves pristine.
It sways and dances, oh so free,
Whispers secrets, just to me.

Its roots are deep, its spirit bright,
In sunny spots, it feels just right.
It dreams of jungles, so they say,
While I forget to water every day!

With every leaf, a giggle grows,
It mocks my gardening woes.
I swear I hear a playful cheer,
As I dash to grab a drink, oh dear!

So here we sit, my friend and I,
In our little oasis, oh my!
A plant with charm and leafy flair,
Together, we make quite the pair!

Flora's Gentle Promise

In a corner, where sunlight spills,
A pot of joy, it gives me thrills.
With stoic grace, it stands so bold,
A wise old sage, or so I'm told.

It nods along to my odd tunes,
Maybe dreaming of wise raccoons.
I wonder if it thinks I'm weird,
For all my chores, it is not teared.

When I forget the watering can,
It plays the part of a chilling fan.
Leaves a bit droopy, a sly little jest,
Saying, "Hey buddy, I need some rest!"

But with a sprinkle, it perks right up,
Like a jester with a funny cup.
We share a laugh—what a delight,
Plant and human, under starlit night!

In the Shade of Verdant Wishes

Beneath the leaves, a world unfolds,
Tales of adventure, of heroes bold.
A sturdy friend with verdant flair,
Does it dream of vacations? I swear!

It giggles at my gardening plight,
As I trip and spill, what a sight!
With every leaf, a chuckle heard,
Is that a smile, or just a bird?

I come with snacks, it leans right in,
A little critter with a cheeky grin.
"Thanks for the crumbs," it seems to say,
As I plop down for a chat each day.

In garden feasts under the sun,
With my leafy buddy, life's such fun!
Together we plot our daily dreams,
An oddball duo, bursting at the seams!

Echoes of the Succulent Soul

With succulent leaves that thrive and shine,
This plant of mine, oh so divine!
It leans to me, gives me a wink,
As I ponder why my flowers stink.

It giggles under moonlit fame,
Whispering secrets and calling my name.
A sage in a planter, so wise and spry,
It even knows when I'm about to cry!

It low-key rolls its leafy eyes,
When I try to bake, but burn the pies.
"Stick to plants," it seems to grin,
While I laugh and think, what a twin!

With every day, our laughter grows,
Sharing life's highs, its silly lows.
A leafy giggle in a sunny space,
Together we bloom, in this playful place!

The Texture of Slow Growth

In a pot, it leans and sways,
Its leaves like tiny hands that play.
With a grin, it stretches slow,
Growing dreams in sunlight's glow.

Every week, it winks and sighs,
Leaves whisper secrets, oh so wise.
Time for tea? It seems to say,
But trust me friend, it sleeps all day.

Roots dig deep, they hold on tight,
Meanwhile, I'm off to win the fight.
Water me? Sure, just a drink,
For all the world, it starts to wink.

Oh little sprout, with dreams so grand,
Life's a drift, not just a stand.
Let's laugh as we both stretch and grow,
In the sunlight's warm, forgiving glow.

Embers of Life in a Leaf

When breezes blow, oh what a show,
A dance of leaves, like tides they flow.
Each leaf a flame, a story told,
In the garden, brave and bold.

Sometimes it sneezes, a little cough,
Releasing dust, oh, please don't scoff!
With filters made of green delight,
It's what keeps things feeling right.

Ants parade, they march with glee,
Something's cooking; can it be me?
A dance-off on the windowsill,
Who knew this leaf had such a thrill?

So here we are, in leafy cheer,
Where tiny giggles fill the sphere.
With each new sprout, a chuckle's found,
In the earth's embrace, we spin around.

The Embrace of Inner Flora

In the corner, a plant with flair,
It greets me daily, without a care.
Its leaves a beacon, soft and bright,
A cozy hug, my true delight.

Under the sun, it sways and beams,
A master chef crafting plant-based dreams.
With soil for soup and sunshine for bread,
It serves up joy, where worries shred.

Every new bud, a wild surprise,
With humor blooming, as time flies.
Sassy stems, so full of sass,
In foliage feuds, they let time pass.

Here's to the flora, oh so wise,
Encouraging giggles, stretching skies.
With laughter bottled in a pot,
I join the dance, I love this lot.

The Resounding Heart of Greenery

Bouncing light upon each leaf,
Every shimmer, a happy grief.
The clock ticks slow, but it laughs away,
Growing jokes on this fine day.

With roots so bold, it waves around,
A leafy band that's homeward bound.
Its whispers echo through the air,
Turns mundane chores to playful flair.

A party of petals, sprouting free,
Inviting neighbors for some tea.
Join the fun, don't miss the show,
Where laughter's seeds are sure to grow.

So here we are, in the hum of green,
In this leafy world, we reign supreme.
With a wink and a chuckle, life's sublime,
Among the greenery, we twirl in time.

A Potted Philosopher's Musings

In a pot, I sit and think,
Wondering if I ought to blink.
Do plants dream of sunny skies?
Or do they giggle at our sighs?

I ponder life in this clay shell,
With climbing vines, I cast my spell.
Should I dance when raindrops drear?
Or meditate with soil near?

The garden gnome shares a grin,
As I discuss the world within.
Do roots hold secrets, deep and vast?
Or do they just wiggle, having a blast?

Oh, to be a leaf on high,
Flirting with bees as they buzz by.
I'll write a book, it's sure to sell,
On the art of living — oh so well!

Guardian Spirits of the Succulent Realm

In the corner, the pot stands tall,
Guardian of plants, watching all.
Do they hold meetings in the night?
Plotting which sunbeam feels just right?

The cacti wear prickles as a crown,
While the aloe boasts of its green gown.
Do they gossip as they grow so spry?
With whispers floating, oh so sly?

Succulents dance with every breeze,
As if the wind brings them some tease.
They share their tales of woe and cheer,
To snails that crawl, and flies that leer.

These sturdy guards with stories thick,
Unravel truths, quirky and slick.
In this realm, joy blooms and beams,
As I, their keeper, weave their dreams.

A Tapestry of Growing Wonders

A tapestry of green unfolds,
Each leaf a secret, waiting, bold.
Do they weave tales of the sun?
Or just throw shade when day is done?

The pot is the stage for this show,
Where roots reach out, creating a glow.
A dance of greens in every hue,
Prancing 'round with a morning dew.

With whispers soft and laughter sweet,
They share their dreams, a rhythmic beat.
Does the fern wish for a starry night?
Or a warm hug from the morning light?

Each sprout tells tales of joy and mirth,
In this patch of green, we find our worth.
Together we thrive, each day anew,
Rooted in love, our bond is true!

Whispered Dreams Among Leaves

In the hush, the leaves all sigh,
Sharing dreams of the big sky.
Do they hope for raindrops fine,
That tickle their edges and vine?

With a nudge, the ferns awake,
Swapping secrets, for laughter's sake.
Do they ponder if bugs take flight?
Or if they'd twirl beneath the night?

A succulent grins with such glee,
Is it thriving or just playing spree?
Leaves giggle and sway with grace,
Turning this pot into a space.

Amidst the chatter, I can't resist,
Joining in this leafy twist.
In dreams of flora, we all unite,
In laughter's glow, our hearts take flight!

Reflections in a Potted World

In a pot so round, so bright,
A plant sits, seeking sunlight.
It wiggles and dances with glee,
I swear it's plotting to flee!

Leaves like tiny, green hats,
Whispering secrets to the cats.
Each sprout has a witty quip,
Ready to take a goofy trip!

I pour my heart into this soil,
While it cackles, just for a foil.
With every drop, it grows so bold,
Mischief in every leaf, behold!

Yet in this potted, leafy space,
I find a friend with a smug face.
Together we jest, we play, we scheme,
Living our best, absurdest dream!

Living Sculpture of Serenity

In the corner, it stands still,
A statue that could use a thrill.
With leaves that bask, in sun's warm hug,
I suspect it's plotting quite a bug!

Every watering a grand affair,
As it sways with an elegant flair.
"Oh, what a lovely drink!" it beams,
While I clumsily pour, spilling dreams!

Should I dance or sing a tune?
Its leaves shake softly, no need for a moon.
It seems to giggle at my plight,
As I fumble in the morning light!

This creature of clay and green so proud,
In its silence, it's really quite loud.
A living statue, my buddy in jest,
Together we laugh, we are truly blessed!

The Elegance of Survival

A leaf pops up as if to say,
"I'm thriving here, hip-hip-hooray!"
With roots so deep, it stands so tall,
Making me question if I'm small!

Its elegance moves like a breeze,
While I trample around, sneezing with ease.
Oh, the grace in every sprout,
Maybe it's telling me to chill out!

Each leaf a shout, a flourish, a cheer,
While I run for coffee, shedding a tear.
Survival's a dance—undeniably true,
Yet somehow, it's always laughing at you!

With every new bud, I sense the vibe,
A comedy show in this green tribe.
Nature's jesters, in pots we reside,
Exchanging giggles and goofy pride!

Radiance in a Leafy Enclosure

Within these walls, a secret blooms,
A leafy ally, with funny costumes.
Basking under the sun's bright gaze,
Flipping its leaves in a sassy haze!

Every morning it greets me so spry,
With a wink from its stem, a greeting high.
"Let's stretch our limbs, let's get some sun!"
I admit, it's more fun than I thought, quite a run!

When I chatter about the world outside,
It nods along, wearing pride.
Together we scheme for snacks on the sill,
Plotting out mischief, thrills to fill!

In this pot, a miracle thrives,
With giggles and green, it completely jives.
Radiance found in this quirky space,
Leaves laughing along, in a silly embrace!

Lush Abyss of Serenity

In the pots, the little greens,
A dance of sprigs with tiny beans.
They wink and nod, so full of cheer,
Whispering secrets for all to hear.

Oh how they stretch, they twist and twirl,
Like rubber bands in a leafy whirl.
With every poke, they seem to say,
'We're here to brighten up your day!'

Each leaf a whisper, a giggle too,
Chasing away the morning dew.
In this haven, all worries cease,
Even the cacti want some peace.

So here's to greens, so bold yet shy,
With funny quirks, they shoot up high.
In this lush land, joy is supreme,
Come join the fun, it's quite the dream!

Tales Written in Green

Once in a pot, a tale unfolds,
Of leaves that act like cheeky fold.
They plot and scheme with crafty glee,
To outsmart you, just wait and see.

A succulent giggles with delight,
As it plans to grow by moonlight.
It stretches long to steal the show,
While other plants are moving slow.

A tiny sprout, with dulcet tones,
Sings songs to pots and wooden bones.
With every twist, they weave their lore,
In this green world, there's always more.

So listen close, and you might find,
The jokes they tell are most unkind,
Yet in their whimsy, we all agree,
They fill our lives with glee, oh me!

Elysian Fields Beneath a Canopy

In fields of green, where laughter sways,
The plants hold court with silly ways.
They trade their gossip on sunny days,
As bees join in the joyful ballet.

Petals flutter, waving hands,
As pots conspire to make new plans.
Each sprout a jester on this stage,
With clever quips that set the gauge.

A rambunctious vine starts to creep,
While others plot without a peep.
Together they scheme, a leafy crew,
Creating pranks, oh what a view!

From stems that chuckle to roots that play,
Their humor sprinkles on everyday.
In this green labyrinth, laughter's free,
Join the merriment, come laugh with me!

Harmony in Every Leaf

Among the greens, a chorus sings,
As leaves sway soft on wispy things.
In harmony, they share their grace,
With love and laughter, they embrace.

A tiny sprout with dreams so grand,
Plans to take over the whole land.
Whispers of victory fill the air,
While daisies plot without a care.

With every drip, the sunshine beams,
In this garden of whimsical dreams.
The pots unite in perfect cheer,
Bringing joy to all who wander near.

So raise your glass, let's toast anew,
To greens that laugh and joke for you.
In every leaf, there's joy to weave,
In this funny world, we all believe!

The Still Breath of Green

In a corner, leaves conspire,
With little whispers, they never tire.
A dance of dust bunnies in the sun,
Making mischief, oh what fun!

They stretch and yawn in morning's glow,
Plotting plans for their leafy show.
With every wiggle, they take a leap,
While my coffee grows cold, I can't help but creep.

Tiny bugs sip on their drink,
While the pot shakes, I start to think.
Who's the master of this home?
Them or me? I'm not alone!

In this realm of leaf and laughter,
Life stirs with colorful chapter after chapter.
As I chuckle at their leafy schemes,
I find joy in these green dreams.

Tales from a Potbound Heart

Locked in a pot, our gossip flows,
With tales of weather and garden woes.
One leaf says, "I'm inching for space!"
While another snaps, "I want a race!"

The roots wriggle, all jammed and tight,
Saying, "Who knew growing could be such a fight?"
They dream of fields, of endless green,
But here they are, just a houseplant scene.

A friendship grows with each sunny day,
We laugh at the birds who come out to play.
"Oh, to be free!" they chirp and cheer,
While I sip my tea, pretending to steer.

But in this pot, we make our stand,
Creating joy, hand in leafy hand.
A cozy life where friends abide,
And laughter echoes in every stride.

Embracing Nature's Resilience

In dirt we trust, we rise and shine,
Pushing through with roots entwined.
Laughing at storms that batter and beat,
"It tickles!" they say, "What a treat!"

Each leaf a story, a tale so grand,
Of sun-soaked days and soft, cool sand.
They twist and twirl in the gentle breeze,
As if performing with perfect ease.

"Oh, look at us! We're quite the show,"
Despite it all, we steal the glow.
With every struggle, we jump and prance,
Reminding the world that life's a dance!

So here we grow, through thick and thin,
With roots like laughter and hearts that grin.
Nature's wise, she's taught us well,
In every crack, a story to tell.

Petals of Fortune

With pots of gold and green galore,
We barter dreams from leaf to floor.
Each sprout a treasure, each bud a laugh,
Calculating the best plant path.

"Oh, what's that?" asks the curious sprout,
"Did someone say it's my turn to shout?"
Petals giggle and green stalks sway,
As they plot and scheme throughout the day.

A sunbeam hits, it's a jackpot bloom,
While I cheer them on from my comfy room.
"Don't forget your roots!" I slyly tease,
As they embrace the warm, gentle breeze.

In the garden of luck, we find our place,
Sharing stories with a bubbly grace.
Petals of fortune, leaves of cheer,
In our plant-filled lives, there's nothing to fear!

Sculpting Moments with Leaves

A succulent sits, plotting scenes,
With leaves so plump, it dreams of greens.
It wiggles, giggles, takes a stance,
Thinking it's won the plant dance chance.

In the sun it thrives, oh what a sight,
Posing like models in golden light.
Whispers to cacti, 'Can you believe?'
While leaves fall off—what a trick up sleeve!

The pot's a stage, it takes a bow,
Insisting, 'Look at me, I'm the star now!'
A paltry remnant, yet so proud,
It yells, 'I'm the funniest in the crowd!'

So here it stands, with a cheeky grin,
All who stop by must laugh and spin.
With every poke or playful tease,
A leafy one-liner, aiming to please!

Serenity in a Terracotta Outpost

In a pot so warm, sits a quirky sprout,
Strikes a pose when the kids shout out.
Its leaves wave like hands in delight,
Saying, 'My daydreams are taking flight!'

With soil on its toes, it joins the fun,
Playing charades under the sun.
Leaves like arms, it stretches wide,
'Who needs a partner? I've got this pride!'

Chasing the sun, it waltzes around,
Every little breeze makes laughter abound.
'Look at me, I'm the dance floor's king!'
Grinning wide, like a silly old thing.

At night it settles, but don't you fret,
For tomorrow's antics, the best are set.
In terracotta, a little balmy,
Life's a comedy—it's downright charming!

From Soil to Spirit

Sprouting up from muddy dreams,
A tiny sprig, or so it seems.
With roots that tickle underground,
It plots a joke that knows no bound.

With each sunrise, it throws a grin,
Swaying lightly, ready to begin.
'Why look so sad?' it whispers soft,
'Come dance with me, let your troubles waft!'

Wiggling leaves like giggling friends,
Creating humor that never ends.
It tells its tales of dirt and sun,
And adds, 'Remember, life's meant for fun!'

So raise a glass to this lively sprout,
With mirth in leaves, there's never doubt.
From soil to spirit, laughter grows,
Cheering us on, wherever it goes!

Harmony Wrapped in Green

In the corner, a plant with flair,
Waves to the world, giving a stare.
'What's so funny?' it seems to ask,
As it dons its leaf-shaped mask.

Its pot, a sage, with wisdom to share,
Whispers truths while tossing hair.
'Life's a garden, make it a show,
Poke some fun and let laughter flow!'

A leaf in the wind, it dances free,
Spreading joy like confetti at a spree.
'Catch me if you can!' it giggles loud,
Wraps its humor in a leafy shroud.

Through ups and downs, it stands so stout,
A comical sage, there's never doubt.
Harmony in green, a riotous scene,
Living its truth in every routine!

Heartbeats of the Earth

In a pot sat a plant, oh so bold,
Sipping on sunlight, never too cold.
It wiggled and jiggled in gentle delight,
Snoring sweet whispers into the night.

Leaves making wishes on soft little sighs,
Telling the world, 'I'm wise and I'm spry!'
With roots sneaking out, they dance in the gloom,
'This soil's my kingdom, I've claimed all the room!'

Neighbors complain, my growing's a spree,
'While he sleeps, let's have a wild tea party!'
Saucers and cups made of leaf and of clay,
FFrolicking foliage, come join the ballet!

With laughter and soil, we sing tunes so sweet,
Inviting the bugs for a lively meet-and-greet.
Now we're a riot, the party must end,
But don't fret dear friend, we'll grow it again!

The Simple Art of Green Nourishment

Happiness is a pot of green fluff,
With a droopy leaf saying, 'I've had enough!'
Just sprinkle some water, not too much please,
Or I'll float off like a leaf from the trees.

Sunbathing loudly, in chubby delight,
Telling the world, 'I'm really quite bright!'
Cookies and cream, my little green friends,
They listen to gossip that never quite ends.

The neighbor's dog barks, all jealous and mean,
'They get all the sunshine, it's totally obscene!'
But I just chuckle, with roots growing wide,
With a wink and a grin, I'm enjoying the ride!

So come join this party, don't leave me alone,
Let's soak up the sillies, like a feather and stone.
With laughter and sunshine, we giggle and sway,
In a world of green dreams, we dance every day!

Unveiling Nature's Secrets

In the hush of the soil, a mystery brews,
Whispering secrets, like the morning dews.
A leaf wore a monocle, looking quite wise,
'Watch closely, my friend, it's all a surprise!'

The roots played hide-and-seek, quite the troupe,
With worms as the judges, they giggled and stooped.
A ladybug surveyed from her towering throne,
'You should have seen it, oh, what a show!'

Petals of laughter burst from the stem,
'Stop pulling my leaves, I'm not your gem!'
The soil laughed louder, its belly in knots,
As plants held a conference, ignoring all thoughts.

'Take it easy!' they cheered, 'We're not in a rush!
Our goal is to grow, not live in a hush!'
So the pot became lively, a wild little spree,
With joy in each giggle, so carefree and free!

Celestial Hues in a Terracotta Vessel

In a vessel of clay, colors twinkle and glow,
Like a painter's palette, putting on a show.
Kaleidoscope leaves that giggle and hum,
Dancing with joy, 'Hey! Look what we've become!'

Underneath the stars, they stretch and they sway,
'The moon's our biggest fan, come join in the play!'
A feathered friend chirps, 'Can I crash the scene?'
The plants giggle back, 'You're part of the dream!'

Blushing and blooming in playful delight,
Roots intertwined, they hold on so tight.
In the warmth of their pot, there's mischief galore,
Breaking out of boundaries, they're always wanting more!

So here's to the colors in terracotta bright,
Where plants become poets, weaving tales in the night.
With laughter as fuel, and joy as their song,
In this garden of dreams, where all of us belong!

Roots Telling Stories

In the soil, whispers grow,
Telling tales of sun and snow.
With a poke and a little twist,
Roots laugh hard—who can resist?

They recount the dance of bugs,
The joy of soil, the happy hugs.
When the rains come pouring down,
They throw a party, wear a crown!

Little tendrils wiggling free,
Join in the fun, it's quite a spree!
Each little root has tales to share,
Of digging deep without a care.

So listen close, they're up to tricks,
In a world of dirt, they play some kicks.
Beneath the earth, they twist and shout,
Roots telling stories—we clap and pout!

In the Company of Green Grace

Oh, to bask in emerald hue,
Where laughter grows and jokes ensue.
With leaves that shimmer in the light,
They tease the breeze, what a delight!

In the presence of grace so bright,
They tell tall tales, take flight at night.
With each flutter, a grin is born,
Smirking at the sleepy morn!

A plant party without a guest,
Leaves are swaying, feeling blessed.
With a shimmy and a sway, they dance,
Oh what fun, come take a chance!

In their company, the humor's grand,
Leaves waving as if to command.
With a chuckle, they grow so free,
Together in joy, come join the spree!

Leaves of Promise

In a sunny spot they lay down roots,
All wearing tiny, leafy suits.
With a wink, they twist and twirl,
Making plans for the next big whirl!

A promise etched in every vein,
To soak up sun, ignore the rain.
Each leaf a venture, bright and bold,
With puns and jokes yet to be told.

In the shade, they share a joke,
Leafy laughter, oh what a poke!
With whispers soft, they strategize,
Plans for scaling the garden skies!

On windy days, the giggles flare,
As they dance without a care.
In the lush green, the fun unfolds,
Leaves of promise, tales retold!

Roots of Past

Buried deep in the earth so grand,
Lie goofy dreams, a silly band.
Old roots chuckle when tales are spun,
Of the times they frolicked—oh what fun!

From hearty grins to wild moonbeams,
They recall laughter echoing in dreams.
In their world of dirt and muck,
They dance along; they're out of luck!

With each shake, a story unfolds,
Of ancient pranks and playful bolds.
Rooted in history, funny and bright,
They shed a tear with sheer delight.

In the underground party, they sway,
Old pals smiling, hip-hip-hooray!
With a tap and a shimmy, they refuse to hide,
Roots of past with joy and pride!

Solitary Symbol of Perseverance

In a pot upon a shelf so high,
Stands a lone succulent, oh my!
With no one near, yet full of glee,
It jocularly plots, 'Just wait and see!'

With each inch gained, it tells a tale,
Of storms and sun, it shall prevail.
In its green heart, it laughs aloud,
'Look at me, I've made you proud!'

As days pass by, it flexes its might,
With quirky leaves that seem to bite.
'You thought I'd wither—how naive!'
Winking softly, 'I won't leave!'

A solitary act, it spins around,
Finding humor in the quiet ground.
Through every struggle, it finds delight,
A silly warrior, holding tight!

The Curves of Contentment

In sunshine warm and friendly light,
A pot sits round, a glorious sight.
Its leaves do stretch and twist with glee,
Whispering secrets, just to me.

With every drink, it gives a grin,
Proclaiming life can just begin.
Wobbling hips, it sways with flair,
As if to say, 'Life's without care!'

A dance of green, oh what a scene,
No worries here, just fun to glean.
"Grow taller, friend!" I cheer aloud,
The plant replies, "I'm feeling proud!"

Its roots get tangled, what a mess!
But who could frown at such success?
In every leaf, a laugh concealed,
A happy world, once fully revealed.

Flourishing in Forgotten Corners

In the back where shadows play,
Lives a beauty, bright and gay.
Dusty shelf, a lost parade,
Yet here it blooms, unafraid.

Old socks piled, a cozy home,
Its laughter echoes, free to roam.
Pruning shears? Oh, what a fright!
"I'll just survive, you know, alright!"

With every sip from a spilled tea,
It giggles softly, "Look at me!"
In the nooks, where life was drear,
It shines like stars, so bright and clear.

A tiny leaf falls with a plop,
"Oops!" it shouts, "I didn't stop!"
Yet blossoms still, with poets' might,
Curtains close on darkened night.

An Offering of Verdant Dreams

Upon my desk, it sways with pride,
Offering dreams from deep inside.
Petals puffed, a jolly grin,
"Join the fun, come take a spin!"

It plots and schemes, oh what a tease,
"Let's ditch this job, go where we please!"
With every growth, a journey planned,
Around the world, we'll take a stand.

A sprinkle here, a dance or two,
In every corner, life's anew.
With each new leaf, it sings a tune,
"Adventure's near, we'll leave by noon!"

Old papers tossed, the desk is clear,
We'll travel far, let's shift a gear.
As laughter fills our leafy dream,
Mischief bubbles like a stream.

The Garden's Inner Voice

In whispers soft, the garden speaks,
A sass so bold, it truly peeks.
"Water me now, or I'll go dry!
Let's share a laugh, oh me, oh my!"

Each leaf a story, bright and loud,
Beneath the sun, it feels so proud.
"See that bug? Oh, what a sight!
Come catch a chat, we'll feel alright!"

From tiny sprout to leafy queen,
In every branch, a laugh is seen.
Yet caution calls, "I'm growing here,
Don't send me off to wilt in fear!"

So stand beside, let's stake our claim,
In every bloom, we'll stake our fame.
With humor sprouting, not a choice—
We revel in the garden's voice.

Echoes of Verdant Life

In the corner, green leaves sway,
Tripping the cat, who thinks it's prey.
Whispers of life in the morning sun,
A dance of delight, let's have some fun.

Chasing shadows, they giggle and roll,
Poking at plants, oh, what a goal!
The pot wobbles, teetering on fate,
And here comes the dog, it's time to skate!

Spongey soils and roots that play,
Each sprout a star in the plant ballet.
They chuckle with glee, a leafy crew,
While I'm left wondering what to pursue.

Napping beneath their leafy shroud,
I dream of vines that grow all proud.
With laughter sprouting from every seam,
Who knew green was such a silly theme?

The Succulent's Serenade

Stuck in a pot, but oh so spry,
They sing little tunes that make me sigh.
Humming and swaying in bright sunlight,
While I sip coffee, their show ignites.

Glistening droplets like jewels of dew,
Each leaf a story, a mishap or two.
With roots like spaghetti, tangled and bold,
They share their secrets — so quirky, so old.

When guests come 'round, I hold my breath,
Watch as they wiggle, who'll win the bet?
A race for the water, a burst of delight,
Our green friends giggling, oh what a sight.

So here's to the lush with a wink and a blush,
Each succulent known for its gentle rush.
They crack me up with their vibrant chat,
Life's little wonders, take time to adapt!

Cradled in Earthen Embrace

Snug in their pots, they cuddle tight,
Gossiping softly under moonlight.
Their leafy whispers, a comical tune,
As they plot and plan the next afternoon.

Oh, how they stretch, with dreams to climb,
Reaching for sunlight, feeling sublime.
Giggling loudly with roots intertwined,
In this earthy cradle, peace combined.

An ant joins the party, a guest of cheer,
Determined to conquer — but full of fear.
With a tumble and spin, they shimmy around,
Creating a ruckus, a joy to be found!

So let's toast the green, in pots they reside,
With mischief and laughter, no need to hide.
In every sprout, there's a tale to tell,
Of earthy delights that we know so well.

Glimmering Leaves of Hope

Glimmers of green in the sunlight's grace,
With laughter and cheer, they fill the space.
Dancing on windowsills, bright and spry,
Each little leaf, a giddy goodbye.

Wiggling roots in a world so wide,
They climb on each other, full of pride.
In the kitchen, they plot a wild spree,
Mixing up flavors for my cup of tea.

Watch them giggle as I tend to stray,
Getting distracted by a wayward bouquet.
They join in the fun, with antics so bold,
Each moment we share, a story retold.

So here's to the leaves, so shiny and bright,
With hopes and laughter, they make life right.
In the garden of dreams, we all stay aglow,
With every small giggle, their spirit will grow.

Spheres of Verdure

In a pot so round and bright,
A little green ball takes flight.
With leaves that giggle under sun,
It thinks it's grown up, oh what fun!

Curled atop a floppy chair,
Plant looks around, beyond compare.
Its thoughts drift off on breezy nights,
Whispering secrets in soft, green bites.

The Botanist's Reverie

A tinkering hand with a pot of clay,
Sings to greens in its quirky way.
Each leaf a laugh, each stem a joke,
In the garden, spirits awoke.

With scissors here and soil so deep,
The botanist dreams while others sleep.
Petals shimmy, roots do dance,
Everyone joins in this leafy trance.

Inspiration Cradled in Green

In the corner, a thumping heart,
Of verdant dreams, a laughing part.
It nudges pens, it nudges books,
Inspiring giggles with wiggly looks.

Wobbling gently, it sips on light,
Plans its mischief by day and night.
Brought to life with a sip of dew,
Each morning greets with something new.

Glistening Companions in Stillness

They gather round, my leafy crew,
With shiny smiles and glistening hue.
In silence, they watch my every move,
Ready to chuckle, ready to groove.

With mirrors reflecting, they plot and scheme,
Each tiny leaf shares a silly dream.
In moments of stillness, they cheer and sing,
My crazy plants, oh what joy they bring!

Shades of Compassion in Resilience

In the corner, a green friend grins,
Telling tales of life beneath thick skins.
Each leaf a hero, in their own way,
They laugh as they grow, come what may.

Water me once, and I'll thrive high,
Show me a light, and I'll reach for the sky.
Rooted in humor, we stretch and bend,
With laughter and patience, we will ascend.

So if you're feeling a little down,
Visit my leaves, let go of that frown.
I'll share my wisdom, leaf by leaf,
Together we'll chuckle, in joy and relief.

Life's a dance, don't take it too seriously,
With friends like me, you'll find it quite cheerily.
In shades of green, we twirl and spin,
Come sip on my joy, let happiness in!

Serenity Angels in Leaves

In the silence, green voices sing,
Whispers of joy that the pot can bring.
Each leaf a mediator, soft and bright,
They giggle at troubles, hidden from sight.

With each little sprout, my heart does bloom,
My friends crack jokes, infusing the room.
When life seems stale, they'll give you a nudge,
Reminding you gently, to never begrudge.

So, when the sky wears a frown, don't you fret,
Come for a chat, I'm not one to forget.
These leafy companions, so silly and spry,
Enlighten the heart, as time flutters by.

With laughter we grow, in sunlight and shade,
Their tales of resilience will never fade.
So lean on me, let's laugh till we drop,
For peace in our hearts will never stop!

Vitality Wrapped in Earth

Under soft soil, where mischief begins,
Roots play hide and seek, oh, what silly sins!
They tickle each other, as they expand,
Cracking up loudly, they've got it all planned.

Life's too short for a pot's dull norms,
Let's frolic in sunshine and dodge the storms.
With a sprinkle of water, our giggles grow,
Dance with me, friends, in this playful show.

Nature's laughter, wrapped snug in green,
A cozy embrace, where joy can be seen.
In this merry madness, jump high, take flight,
For inside this pot, everything feels right.

We sprout little smiles, as vibrant as can be,
Join us in our giggles, oh so carefree.
When life's become heavy, just look down below,
Under the surface, there's laughter to sow!

The Kindness of Green Friends

In a bright room, where sunshine prances,
My leafy pals chuckle, in playful glances.
Bringing joy with each wavering sway,
They keep sadness at bay, hip-hip-hooray!

Potted together, in harmony's cheer,
We trade little secrets, whispered and dear.
When one leaf droops, others jump in to play,
Together we giggle, come what may.

With roots intertwined, we're never alone,
Each quirk and giggle feels like homegrown.
If a cloud hovers, we'll dance through the rain,
Finding the bright side, again and again.

So come join our party, in this green retreat,
Where laughter and kindness share a heartbeat.
In this idyllic patch, we just can't resist,
Celebrating friendship, that'll never be missed!

Quiet Tales of Resilience

In a pot so small, I stretch so tall,
With roots that giggle and leaves that sprawl.
Though I wobble and sway, I stand my ground,
In this game of life, I'm the king, I'm crowned.

Neighbors chat up, they whisper and pine,
"A little more water? Oh, what's the sign?"
I just sip sunshine, while they fret and gush,
I'm thriving in silence, create quite the hush.

Bugs come knocking, I start a parade,
With twirls and shakes, I've mastered the charade.
They worry and fret, but I'm just a sprout,
Turning foes into friends, that's what it's about!

So raise your glass high, give a little cheer,
To the brave little plant, who knows no fear.
With a wink and a nudge, I carry the day,
In this whimsical world, I'll dance and sway.

Spirits of the Potted Oasis

Once in a pot, with a dream so grand,
I spread my plush leaves with a tingly hand.
My friends say I'm lucky, and I humbly grin,
Just waiting for sunshine, let the fun begin!

At night I gossip with my leafy friends,
Sharing tales of light and how the day ends.
"Did you see that bug? He thought he could snack!"
We laugh till we wilt, and then bounce back!

When rain ticks my leaves, like a jazzy beat,
We sway and we twist, tapping our green feet.
In our little oasis, the spirits unite,
"We're dancing with droplets, what a joyous sight!"

So here meow the vibes, just sprinkle a cheer,
In the world of houseplants, there's nothing to fear.
We flourish and flourish, each leaf a delight,
In our potted paradise, everything feels right.

The Subtle Dance of Photosynthesis

In the corner of sunshine, I set the show,
With my little green blades, watch the energy flow.
Photosynthesis, oh what a thrill!
Turning sunlight to snacks, I'm the queen of the grill!

The sun gives a wink, and I shimmy just right,
With pigments and smiles, I glow in the light.
My friends look all jealous, with envy they stare,
"Well, I'll just grow brighter, if you dare!"

The air is my stage, where I twirl and sway,
Breathing in giggles, exhaling all gray.
"So what if I'm rooted? I can still dance free,
In this comedic ballet, just watch and see!"

So here's to the greens with their silent glee,
Basking in laughter, we flourish with ease.
In this lively affair, let me tip my hat,
To the joyful plants, we're where it's at!

Soft Shadows on Sunlit Soil

At the edge of the pot, I plot my grand scheme,
Soft shadows at play, like a whimsical dream.
The sun's got my back, and the soil's quite soft,
With every slow wiggle, my laughter takes off.

The gardener whispers, "Now don't be so bold,"
But if they only knew, I'm a sight to behold!
With tiny green pranks, I'll nuzzle and tease,
In this sunlit theater, I do what I please.

Each time it rains down, like a giggly show,
I twinkle and shimmer, letting happiness flow.
My friends in their pots, we chuckle along,
Creating a symphony, a potted plant song.

So bring in the light, let the shadows play tricks,
In this cozy little spot, where laughter afflict.
With roots intertwined, we're the best of the crew,
In this world of green magic, there's always room for two!

A Reverie of Succulent Shadows

In a pot so round, a green delight,
Leaves so thick, they laugh at the night.
They wiggle and jiggle in the sun's warm glow,
Whispering secrets that only they know.

A leaf took a dive, off the edge it flew,
"Look at me! I'm airborne!" it proudly cooed.
But landed with grace, on another's back,
All were in stitches, the leaves shared a crack.

A root had a dream to swim in the sea,
"Oh, how refreshing!" it shouted with glee.
The pot shook with laughter, held tight with glee,
As branches crack jokes in the sun's jubilee.

With paws from a cat tiptoeing by,
"Oh no! It's a monster!" the leaves all cry.
But it was just Mittens, confused and bemused,
Stealing the spotlight, unfazed and amused.

Life's Quiet Abode.

In the corner of the room, where sunlight beams,
A squad of green buddies plot silly schemes.
They throw wild parties when no one is here,
And dance like they just drank a pint of root beer.

When dusk creeps in, the leaves start to sway,
Pretend they're a band on a variety day.
The pots are the stage, the soil is the crowd,
As they belt out their tunes, happy and loud.

A shadow approaches, they freeze in a fright,
Is it danger or just someone turning on light?
"Oh no, it's the human! Quick, act like a plant!"
But giggles escape, it's too hard to recant!

They dream of their vacation to sunny Bali,
Where they'd make friends with a tall, goofy galley.
But for now, they laugh in their cozy abode,
Living life fully, in their green leafy road.

Green Whispers in Clay

In the clay, a gathering of green little minds,
With whispers of laughter, and very few binds.
They pipe up with tales from the last rainy night,
Of chasing their shadows till well out of sight.

One leaf claims to have hopped on a breeze,
Said it soared like an eagle, all graceful with ease.
But a nearby petal shouts, "That's a tall tale!"
Last I saw you, you were stuck in a pail!

They struck up a bet on who could grow bigger,
Each leaf shot up high, like a playful jigger.
But when all had sprouted, they laughed and did see,
It's not about height, it's about unity!

So they toast with their roots, a clink for good fun,
In their pot of dreams, they all shine like the sun.
With giggles and jests, they live with no care,
In their whimsical world, free as fresh air.

Secrets of the Succulent

In a garden of gems, where humor is shared,
The stout little ones are quite clever and dared.
They cast little glances and practice their winks,
Swapping their tales over sugary drinks.

A prickly adventurer boasts of a fight,
With a rogue garden gnome in the dead of the night.
But all know too well, he just rolled on the grass,
And slept through the brawl while his pals had a blast.

A succulent soul whispered, "I saw it all,
With roots in a tangle, my buddies, they'd stall!"
But sharing that secret, oh what a delight,
They giggled and snickered till morning's first light.

So here's to the leaves, who plot and they scheme,
In a world full of laughter, fulfilling their dream.
They teach us to enjoy, and never feign dread,
For life's a wild ride, filled with joy, not just bread.

Roots of a Tranquil Mind

In a pot so wide, I sit with glee,
Wondering if I'm a shrub or a tree.
My leaves like coins, they sparkle and shine,
Should I start charging for hugs? That's fine!

Water me a little, then let me be,
Too much affection and I may flee.
As the sun beams bright, I stretch my arm,
Hoping my charm doesn't cause any harm.

When friends come over, they can't help but stare,
With my showy attire, I've got flair!
Do they think I'm wise or just quite bizarre?
Watch me grow tall— I'm a leaf star!

With roots so deep and dreams so grand,
I ask for a dance, take a chance, take a stand.
In the garden of laughter, I grow ever high,
Roots of a mind that's ready to fly.

Gardens of Unspoken Secrets

In the secret garden where giggles bloom,
I whisper to flowers, dispelling the gloom.
They giggle back sweetly with every breeze,
Telling me tales of bees and their tease.

My neighbor's cat thinks he owns my patch,
Dancing with shadows in quite the catch.
With snaps in the air and a leap so spry,
I think he just dreams he can give it a try!

The soil beneath holds secrets galore,
Like where all my missing socks went before.
I plant my worries, watch them take flight,
They sprout into jokes that tickle at night.

So, here in this haven where laughter grows,
I chat with the veggies; everyone knows,
We weave up our stories with roots intertwined,
In gardens where whispers make sunshine combined.

The Bounty of Tender Care

With a sprinkle of love and a dash of cheer,
I nurture the leaves that hold me dear.
They stretch up to greet the light of the day,
While I giggle and dance in my own leafy way!

A cookie for me? Oh, I must not indulge,
But my succulent friends they stare and they bulge!
I sigh and I laugh, 'What a funny affair!
Can plants have sweet dreams? I'd like to declare!'

When the gardener cackles at weeds in the sun,
We cheer on the flowers; oh, we're all having fun!
From pots of clay, a banquet of flair,
With veggies so stylish, it's hard to compare!

So here's to the bounty, the harvest of smiles,
Where laughter is plenty, and joy spans for miles.
Tender care shared among pals that we trust,
In the realm of green, it's a must to adjust!

Greening the Gaps of Life

In the fast lane racing, I find a small pot,
That calms all my chaos, nice and hot.
A cuddle of green in a world of gray,
Takes my worries and sweeps them away.

Between gardener's tasks, there's giggling galore,
We patch every pothole, we laugh and explore.
As dirt on my hands adds a shade of delight,
I ponder if vegetables can dance in the night!

Each leaf a reminder to take things in stride,
While snickering weeds act like they're my guide.
In the gaps of my day, tiny spirits unite,
Turning simple moments into pure delight.

With laughter and growth filling up every space,
I fill up my heart, finding solace and grace.
So, here's to the humor that plants can impart,
Greening the gaps while we create from the heart!

Fables of the Verdant World

In pots of green where wonders sprout,
The secrets of life begin to shout.
Tiny leaves with a wink and a grin,
Whisper tales of where they've been.

They dance in the breeze, oh what a sight,
Claiming the sun with all of their might.
While cactus looks on with envy and sass,
The succulent crew just fluffs up the grass.

Echoes of Soft Growth

Through sunlight's glow and rain's soft kiss,
The green brigade plots its leafy bliss.
One's taking naps, another's on a quest,
In their world, it's all just a jest.

A sage leaf shouts, 'Don't miss the show!'
'Look at that worm! It's puttin' on a low!'
Laughter erupts from the garden's delight,
As petals giggle into the night.

Petals of Dreams

In a cup of sunshine, tucked away tight,
Dreams of green take their playful flight.
The daisies giggle, the violets cheer,
While the ferns hide secrets, oh so dear.

They plot adventures, they scheme with glee,
A dance party! Just wait and see!
In the wildest of dreams, they're never alone,
The garden's a stage, and they're in the zone.

Leaves of Reality

Reality check! The leafy crew sings,
With potting soil boots and tiny green wings.
They'll conquer the kitchen, munching on crumbs,
A secret rebellion, oh how it hums!

'Let's raindance!' says Fern with a gleam,
While Rosemary plots chocolate ice cream.
In a world made of soil, they plot and play,
Making mischief in their own special way.

Synergy of Earth and Sky

Between earth and sky, they spin a grand tale,
Of sunlit adventures, on a joyous scale.
The chubby leaves wobble, they giggle with cheer,
As they plot their escape from the ground, my dear!

On cloud-walking whims, they frolic and sway,
Chasing the wind as they laugh and play.
In a world of soil, they feel so alive,
With roots in the ground, watch their spirits thrive!

Solace Found in Thickened Leaves

In a corner, tall and stout,
My potted friend prances about.
With thickened leaves and no care,
Who knew a plant could be quite so rare?

Sunlight trickles, a gentle tease,
As I sip my coffee, aiming to please.
She stretches up like she owns the space,
While I'm just here, in my pajama embrace.

Every morning, she's there to greet,
In this odd duo, I find my seat.
We share the room, as if to say,
Let's banter on through another day.

With each new leaf, I tell her a joke,
She sways a little, laughing bespoke.
In this plant life, nothing's too hard,
Just me and my buddy, a garden backyard.

Nurturing Growth in Etched Serenity

Nurturing dreams with a dash of glee,
My green companion chats back with me.
With a wink and a shake of her limbs,
Life seems brighter, the outlook brims.

Soil's a-squish in every nook,
Her roots must dance in the cozy book.
I read her tales of sun and shade,
And wonder what mischief she's already made.

With each sprout, a comet's flight,
On my desk, she becomes the highlight.
"Do plants have parties?" I giggle and muse,
"Is there a potluck with herbs in the blues?"

In a life so simple, no need to rush,
She rolls her leaves, igniting my hush.
Together we thrive with a chuckle and grin,
Our bond is solid; it's a win-win!

Melodies of the Indoor Green

In the twilight, melodies are found,
Whispers of green in a gentle sound.
My pal stands tall, a maestro in clay,
Conducting the breeze in a jazzy display.

With every leaf, a note so sweet,
A symphony blooms beneath my feet.
I clap for the show, while she nods with pride,
A duet of laughter, no secrets to hide.

The sunlight shifts, painting her bright,
She pirouettes gently, a whimsical sight.
I join her dance, a shuffling pair,
Turning my living room into a fair.

In this concert of leaves, joy is supreme,
Her touch is soft, like a calming dream.
As saplings and smiles twirl in the space,
Together we sing, in our little place.

Laidback Dreams of Surrounding Nature

In the realm of pot and soil,
My leafy friend deserves the spoils.
She lounges back like royalty,
While I fetch snacks with a knack for folly.

"Should we host a chill plant retreat?"
Her leaves quiver as if to greet.
With moss for blankets, and sun for light,
We'll sip on dew till it's night.

Nature peeks through the windowpane,
With whispers of breezes, no room for pain.
Laughter echoes in our cozy nook,
In this leafy space—who needs a book?

So here we stay, my buddy and me,
Crafting tales of leaves and glee.
With no regrets, we share our space,
Together we dream, in this calm embrace.

Green Spheres of Hope

In a pot with a smile wide,
Little spheres in green reside.
Poking out from their cozy nest,
Waiting for their leafy jest.

Each day they wiggle, twist, and turn,
Sharing secrets, slowly learn.
My cat thinks they're her new best friends,
As each leaf bends and pretends.

With sunlight's hug, they grow so tall,
But my watering can's the real brawl.
I spill a little, laugh out loud,
Their happy dance makes me so proud.

Though they know mischief, they are prim,
Convincing me that I can't swim.
In the sea of soil they dive and sway,
Growing dreams in their own silly way.

Whispers of a Leafy Sanctuary

Once upon a leafy lore,
Plants whispered dreams from floor to floor.
They chat about the bugs they see,
While plotting how to steal my tea.

In the corner, one sneezed 'achoo!'
Dropping soil like a secret crew.
A tiny leaf with flair so bold,
Winks at me, a tale retold.

Every morning, they have a peek,
At my breakfast, oh so sleek.
With avocado toast in view,
I swear they're plotting what to chew.

When I forget to give them treats,
They sulk and pout in their green seats.
But catch them laughing in the light,
A leafy crew, a joyous sight!

The Silent Growth Beneath

In the shadows of the pot,
Little roots are growing hot.
They wiggle 'neath the happy soil,
Like dancing feet in a joyful toil.

Silly whispers from the ground,
Make the pot feel safe and sound.
"Do not disturb! We're quite at play!"
As I water them, they sway.

With every inch of growth they gain,
They giggle softly, quite insane.
Pretending not to seek the sun,
Oh, the games of roots—what fun!

When the night falls, what a show!
Roots pull pranks we'll never know.
In silent laughter, they explore,
Creeping up, they always want more.

Cradled in Earth's Embrace

In cozy dirt, they snuggle tight,
Dreaming of their leafy height.
With every inch, they lose their chill,
As they stretch and laugh at will.

They're plotting ways to steal my socks,
Wearing them like leafy frocks.
Each new sprout a tiny prank,
Cackling gently, "This is dank!"

As I nap, they hold a ball,
Playing tag upon the wall.
Good slopes of soil, a joyful ride,
In earth's embrace, they can't hide.

With every tender new delight,
They giggle softly in the night.
These little greens, such sweet affair,
Make my home a happy lair.

www.ingramcontent.com/pod-product-compliance
Lightning Source LLC
Chambersburg PA
CBHW070311120526
44590CB00017B/2632